EARTH SCIENCE ROCKS!
Fossils

by Chris Bowman

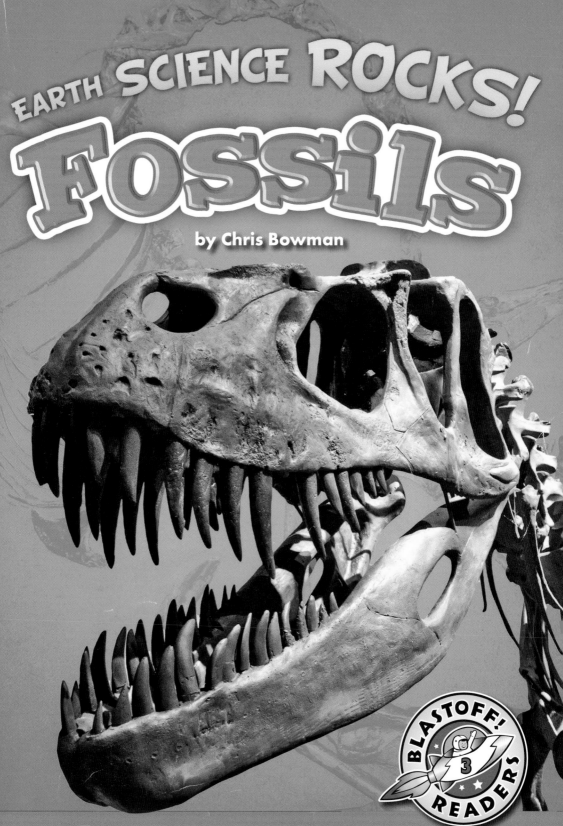

BELLWETHER MEDIA • MINNEAPOLIS, MN

BLASTOFF!
3
READERS

Note to Librarians, Teachers, and Parents:

Blastoff! Readers are carefully developed by literacy experts and combine standards-based content with developmentally appropriate text.

Level 1 provides the most support through repetition of high-frequency words, light text, predictable sentence patterns, and strong visual support.

Level 2 offers early readers a bit more challenge through varied simple sentences, increased text load, and less repetition of high-frequency words.

Level 3 advances early-fluent readers toward fluency through increased text and concept load, less reliance on visuals, longer sentences, and more literary language.

Level 4 builds reading stamina by providing more text per page, increased use of punctuation, greater variation in sentence patterns, and increasingly challenging vocabulary.

Level 5 encourages children to move from "learning to read" to "reading to learn" by providing even more text, varied writing styles, and less familiar topics.

Whichever book is right for your reader, Blastoff! Readers are the perfect books to build confidence and encourage a love of reading that will last a lifetime!

This edition first published in 2015 by Bellwether Media, Inc.

No part of this publication may be reproduced in whole or in part without written permission of the publisher. For information regarding permission, write to Bellwether Media, Inc., Attention: Permissions Department, 5357 Penn Avenue South, Minneapolis, MN 55419.

Library of Congress Cataloging-in-Publication Data

Bowman, Chris, 1990- author.
  Fossils / by Chris Bowman.
    pages cm. – (Blastoff! Readers. Earth Science Rocks!)
  Summary: "Developed by literacy experts for students in kindergarten through grade three, this book introduces fossils to young readers through leveled text and related photos"– Provided by publisher.
  Audience: Ages 5-8.
  Audience: K to grade 3.
  Includes bibliographical references and index.
  ISBN 978-1-60014-979-5 (hardcover : alk. paper)
  1. Fossils–Juvenile literature. 2. Paleontology–Juvenile literature. I. Title.
  QE714.5.B69 2014
  560–dc23
                                            2014002366

Text copyright © 2015 by Bellwether Media, Inc. BLASTOFF! READERS and associated logos are trademarks and/or registered trademarks of Bellwether Media, Inc. SCHOLASTIC, CHILDREN'S PRESS, and associated logos are trademarks and/or registered trademarks of Scholastic Inc.

Printed in the United States of America, North Mankato, MN.

Table of Contents

What Are Fossils?

Fossils are pieces or marks of **ancient** life. They are thousands to billions of years old!

Some fossils are the **remains** of plants and animals. Others are just **traces** of them.

Fossils are found all over the world. Most are **preserved** in **sedimentary rock**.

Some are frozen in ice that never melts. Others are stuck in hardened **amber**.

How Fossils Form

Few plants and animals become fossils. Most **decay** or are eaten. Remains must be buried to become fossils. That way they do not break down.

Earth's Layers

Earth is made up of the inner core, outer core, mantle, and crust. Fossils are found in the crust.

crust

mantle

outer core

inner core

Sediments cover the remains. They keep bones, shells, and leaves from being damaged.

Fossil Cycle

1

The sand or mud slowly sinks.
Over time, it hardens into rock.

3

Eventually **minerals** enter the preserved remains. The bones, shells, and leaves slowly become rock, too. They have turned into fossils.

In time, the rock around the fossils **erodes**. The fossils move to the surface.

4

Types of Fossils

Fossils of bones, shells, and leaves are called body fossils. They are the remains of living things.

body fossil

trace fossil

Trace fossils are marks of living things. Animal tracks, eggshells, and nests are examples.

Mold fossils form when rock keeps the shape of a plant or animal.

mold fossil

cast fossil

Sometimes minerals fill the mold. These fossils are called **cast** fossils.

Fossils as Clues

Scientists who study fossils are called **paleontologists**. They dig up fossils. Then they figure out their age.

They add the fossils to the **fossil record**. This is to track how plants and animals change over time.

Hunting for Fossils

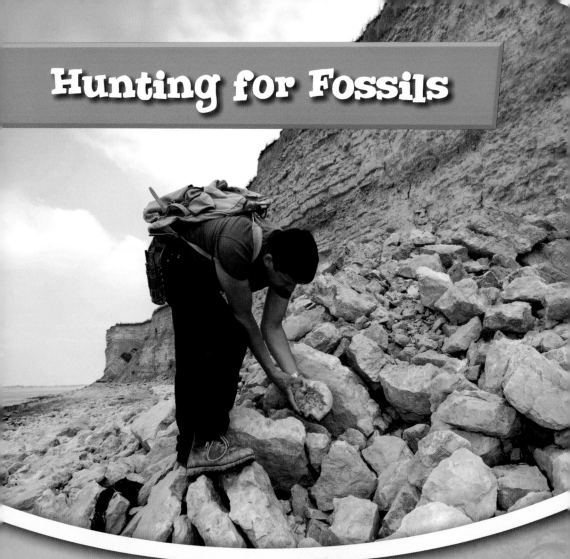

The best places to look for fossils are areas that used to be underwater. **Quarries** and coastlines are good spots, too. Dig in to discover the past!

Be a Paleontologist!

What you need:

clay   plaster of paris   shell

1. Press the shell into the clay and then remove. Make sure the shell's shape and details show.

2. Mix the plaster of paris with water. Then pour that into the mold.

3. Wait for the plaster to harden. Then pull it out of the clay. You have just made a fossil!

Glossary

amber—a sticky, yellow substance made by some trees; sometimes bugs and pollen fossilize in hardened amber.

ancient—very old

cast—a mold fossil that is filled

decay—to rot or break down

erodes—wears away

fossil record—the collection of fossils that people have found; the fossil record shows how life on Earth has changed over time.

minerals—solid substances found in nature

mold—a fossil that is the stamp of a living thing

paleontologists—scientists who study fossils

preserved—kept in its original shape

quarries—large rock pits

remains—the bodies of dead plants and animals

sedimentary rock—rock formed by material on the bottom of a body of water

sediments—materials that settle on the bottom of bodies of water

traces—marks left by living things

To Learn More

AT THE LIBRARY
Petersen, Christine. *Fantastic Fossils*. Edina, Minn.:
ABDO Pub. Co., 2010.

Spilsbury, Richard and Louise. *Fossils*. Chicago, Ill.:
Heinemann Library, 2011.

Walker, Sally M. *Figuring Out Fossils*. Minneapolis,
Minn.: Lerner Publications, 2013.

ON THE WEB
Learning more about fossils
is as easy as 1, 2, 3.

1. Go to www.factsurfer.com.

2. Enter "fossils" into the search box.

3. Click the "Surf" button and you will see a
   list of related web sites.

With factsurfer.com, finding more
information is just a click away.

Index

The images in this book are reproduced through the courtesy of: Marques, front cover; alice-photo, p. 4; Pablo Hidalgo, p. 5; Jaroslav Moravcik, pp. 6-7; Phil Robinson/ age fotostock/ SuperStock, p. 7; Ecoprint, p. 8; Webspark, p. 9; Teguh Mujiono, pp. 10, 11, 12, 13; Allocricetulus, p. 14; David Parsons, p. 15; Eduardo Rivero, pp. 16, 17; Science Source, p. 19; Pascal Goetgheluck/ Science Source, p. 20; tescha555, p. 21 (left); imagedb, p. 21 (middle); Alexander Raths, p. 21 (right).